The

Here is the Griffin.

The sun shone
in the blue sky.
The Griffin flew across
the blue sea.

The Griffin looked down,
as he flew across the sea.
He saw a ship.
He flew down to look
at the ship.

The sails of the ship were red and gold.
The ship had a flag.
The flag was green and gold.

The sun shone
on the Griffin,
as he flew down
to look at the ship.
The sailors on the ship
looked up,
and saw the Griffin.

The Griffin saw
a little island,
away across the sea.
He left the ship,
and flew across the sea
to the island.

The sailors
saw the island.
The ship sailed
to the island.

A sailor left the ship,
and went on to
the island.

A green sea-dragon
was hidden on the island.

The sea-dragon
saw the ship
sail to the island.

He saw the sailor
on the island.
He flew across the island.

The sailor looked up.
He saw the sea-dragon.
He ran back to the ship.
He ran and ran and ran.

The Griffin flew across
the island.
He looked down.
He saw the sailor,
as the sailor ran back
to the ship.
He saw the sea-dragon.

The Griffin flew down on to the sea-dragon's back.

The sailor ran to the ship.
The sea-dragon flew
up into the sky,
with the Griffin
on his back.

The sea-dragon
flew away,
across the sea,
with the Griffin
on his back.

The sun was setting.
The ship left the island.
The sailors sailed away,
away across the sea.
The Griffin left
the sea-dragon,
and flew back
to the island.